101
AFFIRMATIONS
FOR
TEENAGERS

Compiled by
the Editors of Group Publishing

Group®

101 Affirmations for Teenagers
Copyright © 1993 Group Publishing, Inc.

First Printing

Credits
Edited by Michael Warden
Cover designed by Bob Fuller
Cover photograph by Joel Grimes

Library of Congress Cataloging-in-Publication Data
101 affirmations for teenagers / compiled by the Editors of Group Publishing ; [edited by Michael Warden].
      p.   cm.
   ISBN 1-55945-176-9
   1. Church work with teenagers. 2. Teenagers—Religious life.
3. Teenagers—Conduct of life. I. Warden, Michael D. II. Editors of Group Publishing. III. Title: One hundred and one affirmations for teenagers.
BV4447.A15   1993
268'.433—dc20
                                                    92-44531
                                                         CIP

Printed in the United States of America

CONTENTS

PART 2:

PART 3:

PART 4:

INTRODUCTION

By the time kids reach their teenage years, chances are they've become experts at filtering the messages they hear from others. Messages that reinforce what kids already think of themselves are easily received. But messages that contradict kids' beliefs about their lives are just as easily discarded.

Of course, this would be a handy tool if all kids truly believed they were as wonderful as God thinks they are. Then just about every negative message they heard would be nimbly caught and thrown into oblivion. Unfortunately, this rarely happens. Because in real life, many teenagers believe they aren't valuable—that they aren't even worth wasting a compliment on.

Sometimes encouraging words *do* break through kids' defenses:

"I really enjoy spending time with you."

"You have a great way of having fun, no matter what you're doing."

"I really appreciate the way you value honesty."

"You are special."

When those all-important words do break into kids' hearts, a new world opens for them— a world where they don't have to perform for love or be afraid of rejection, because they *know* they're truly valuable to God and to others.

Negative messages attack kids from many different sources—Mom, Dad, siblings, school friends, teachers, television, politicians, and even the church. With all these sources telling kids what's wrong with them, who's going to tell them what's *right* with them?

Well, you can.

101 Affirmations for Teenagers is designed to help you creatively combat the false beliefs kids have about themselves. It also gives wonderful suggestions for ways kids can affirm others and help push back the negative messages to make room for the truth: "God created you... and you're special."

Those words are what this book is all about. Use *101 Affirmations for Teenagers* to break kids' defenses and to get to their hearts. Once you do, their lives will never be the same.

HOW TO USE THIS BOOK

As you use the affirmations in this book, consider these guidelines:

1. Set an example of love and acceptance. Before you can expect kids to seriously give and receive affirmation, you must learn how to model it for them. Speak positively about kids any chance you get. Avoid all putdowns. Be vulnerable with them so they can see that *you* know God loves you. Then kids can begin to believe God loves them, too.

2. Encourage kids to be positive. When doing an affirmation, discourage kids from poking fun at one another. Challenge them to focus only on the positive activity you're doing.

3. Encourage kids to be direct and specific. When kids are affirming one another, challenge them to speak directly to the person they're affirming and to be specific in their affirmation. For example, "Francis, I really admire your ability to have fun no matter what's going on in your life" is better than "I like his outlook on life."

4. Encourage kids to maintain eye contact. Especially when kids are receiving affirmation, encourage them to look into the eyes of the person affirming them. It may feel uncomfortable at first, but it helps kids believe that what that person is saying about them is true.

5. Encourage kids to avoid using comparisons or focusing on unchangeable features. For example, kids shouldn't say things such as "You're a lot better than I am at math" or "You have such beautiful hair." Comments such as these make kids feel they're special only because they perform well against others or because of a personal feature they can't change. Encourage kids to focus on character traits and actions instead.

By following these guidelines and using the ideas in this book, you'll help kids break down negative beliefs about themselves and help them begin to see their lives with new eyes—the eyes of unconditional love and acceptance.

PART 1

TEENAGERS TO TEENAGERS

AFFIRMATIONS FOR TEENAGERS TO GIVE ONE ANOTHER

A IS FOR AWESOME!

Set out a variety of colored pens, markers, crayons, and pencils. Give kids each a 2-foot square of newsprint and allow them to creatively write their name at the top.

Then have kids each print the alphabet in large letters down the left side of the paper. Tape the papers to the walls.

When all the papers are taped, have kids roam around, filling in affirming adjectives that describe the person named at the top of the paper. Allow only one adjective per letter of the alphabet. Encourage creativity and variety, particularly on letters such as Q and X!

Keep the papers on the walls for a few weeks, then allow kids to take them home as permanent reminders of their good qualities—from A to Z!

2 AFTER I'M GONE

Explain to kids that Huck Finn faked his own death and then heard what others said about him after he was "gone." Discuss briefly what it would be like to lose a good friend.

Ask:

● **If you were responsible for writing your friend's eulogy, what would you write?**

Explain that a eulogy is a thoughtful remembrance of a person's life, given after his or her death. Tell kids you would like each person to thoughtfully write a eulogy for another member of the group. Make sure that everyone has an assignment so that no one gets left out. Encourage kids to highlight what good things their assigned people brought to others' lives and what made him or her special and unique. Ask them to finish with a single statement that sums up the life-philosophy of their friend as they observed it.

When everyone is ready, have kids each read their eulogy. Applaud kids for their sensitivity and thoughtfulness.

Ask:

● **Why does it seem like we have to wait until we're dead before others will tell us how awesome we are?**

● **How can we break that "code of silence" here in our youth group?**

Have kids each give the eulogy they wrote to their assigned person. Encourage kids to keep their eulogies in a prominent place at home as a reminder to tell people how awesome they are.

AMAZING PREDICTIONS

Say: **The future can be pretty scary since we don't know what's going to happen. Let's take a peek into a possible future for you.**

One at a time, call each person forward to take a seat in a chair you've designated as a "time machine." As each person sits in the time machine, have the other group members offer positive suggestions for what the future could hold for that person, based on known interests and the person's positive qualities. For example, someone might say, "I see you becoming a famous writer because you're so creative with words."

BAG-O-ESTEEM

Give kids each a grocery-size paper bag. Supply scissors and have kids cut out holes for eyes, nose, and mouth. Give kids markers and have them write their names on their bags. Then have kids each put the bag over their head. Tell kids to go around the room and write notes of encouragement or draw positive "affirmation" pictures on other people's bags. After a while, have kids remove their bags and read them. Ask:

- **Why is acceptance and affirmation so important?**
- **Should the way we look influence whether or not we're accepted or encouraged? Why or why not?**
- **To be a part of a unified group, why is it important to know who you are as an individual?**
- **Why is it important for other people to know who you are as an individual?**

5 BAG OF GOODIES

Dump a wide assortment of candies into a paper bag. Have the group form a circle and tell kids to each pull out a piece of candy from the bag.

One at a time, have kids give their candy away to someone else in the room. As they give their candy, have them complete this statement: "You're like a (name the candy) because..." For example, someone might say, "You're like a Tootsie Roll because your smiles last a long time."

If a person receives more than one piece of candy, he or she must give away all extra pieces (using the same affirmation process) until everyone in the room has one piece of candy.

Close by eating your candy together.

BALLOON BOUQUETS

Purchase enough different-colored balloons and string so each person can have five. Also, rent a tank of helium sufficient to inflate that number of balloons.

When kids arrive, give them each five balloons of different colors, five strings, and a marker. Have kids inflate their balloons with helium and tie the strings on the ends.

Have kids each write their name on their five balloons and let them float up to the ceiling (don't do this activity in a gym!). Gather the group together and explain the activity.

Say: **On "go," I want each of you to write as many encouraging notes of appreciation on as many balloons as possible. Be honest and positive in your notes. For example, you might write, "You're a great friend" or "I'm glad you're in the group." Keep track of the number of notes you write by marking your hand with slash marks. You have four minutes. Go!**

Play fast-paced music while kids are writing. When time is up, find the winner (or winners) and pronounce them Mr. or Ms. Encouragement. Have kids gather their balloons and take them home—a bouquet of encouraging balloons!

7 BAND-AIDS

Give each person two small Band-Aid strips. Tell kids to stick their Band-Aid strips on other group members while completing this statement: "You always heal my hurts because you..."

8 BREAD OF LIFE

Show kids a solid loaf of bread. Form a circle and break off a piece of the bread. As you hold up the piece of bread, tell how one person in the circle has brought the new life of Christ to your life—without mentioning the person's name. When you're finished telling about the person, eat your piece of bread and give the loaf to the person you described.

Have that person repeat the process, passing the loaf to another person in the room.

Continue until everyone has received the loaf. Then give each person another piece from the loaf and ask:

● **How is the church like a loaf of bread?**

● **How are we like food in one another's lives?**

● **How can we nourish one another more?**

Eat the bread pieces together and then pray for God to build unity in your group and make you all part of the same "bread" of life.

CHARACTER CARDS

On a stack of 3×5 cards, write as many positive qualities as you can think of (one quality per card). It's okay if you repeat some qualities but try to create an assortment. Use traits such as "friendly," "caring," "wise," "helpful," and "loving." Make enough cards so each person in the group can have three.

Form a circle and have kids sit on the floor. Give each person three cards, face-down. Ask kids not to look at the cards until you explain the activity.

Say: **On your cards, I've written different positive character traits. Your goal is to give each card to someone in the group who has the quality written on the card. Give the cards away by placing them face-down in front of the people you give them to. Once a card has been given away, it cannot be touched or looked at until the end of the activity. No person may receive more than three cards.**

After asking if everyone understands the instructions, have kids start giving away their cards. Once all the cards have been given away, have kids each look at the cards they've been given. Go around the circle and have kids read their cards. As they read each card, have group members tell how they've seen that quality demonstrated in that person's life.

10 CHRISTMAS COMPARISONS

Gather kids together during the Christmas season for a special affirmation time. Meet in a home that's decked with Christmas decorations—everything from lights to fruitcake. Form a circle and have kids take turns sitting in the center of the circle.

For each person sitting in the center, have group members tell that person some positive reasons that he or she is like a particular Christmas object. For example someone might say, "Jerry, you're like the lights on the tree because you have such a colorful and cheery personality."

Allow each person one minute in the center and then have that person trade with someone new. Continue until each person has sat in the center.

Close the time together by reminding kids that we are all gifts from God to one another. Then sing a favorite Christmas carol.

COLLAGE CREATIONS

S et out a stack of newspapers and magazines, construction paper, scissors, glue, and markers. Have kids write their names on slips of paper and drop them into a hat.

Explain to the group that you're going to do a fun, cut-and-paste activity. Have kids each draw a name out of the hat and keep the name drawn a secret. With the materials available, have each person cut out pictures, words, and letters to create a collage that positively describes the person whose name has been drawn. Encourage creativity and compliments! Have the creator write the name of the person described on the back of the collage.

After everyone is finished, have group members guess who's described in each of the collages. Once a collage's subject is discovered, have the creator explain the collage before presenting it to the appropriate person.

12 DOLLAR DELIGHTS

Ask kids to each donate one dollar to complete this activity. Take the group to a mall (or a drugstore), assign a secret partner (someone in the group) to each person, and have kids fan out into the mall (or store) and use their dollars to buy something for their partner.

Tell kids the item must in some way communicate a positive quality that the secret partner has. For example, Josie might buy Bill a water gun because he's always refreshing the people around him.

Have kids come back together at a specific time to present the gifts to their secret partners. End the activity with a group hug.

13 FEATHER IN YOUR CAP

Give kids each a large elastic band and two feathers. Have kids place the elastic around their heads like a headband. Then have kids each go to someone else and place a feather in his or her band. As they give away the feathers, have kids each tell the person about a quality that person has that they ad-mire. Tell kids they must give away both feath-ers. If students receive more than two feathers, they must give the extras to other people in the group. The activity is over when each person has two feathers in his or her headband.

After the activity, ask:

● **What differences have we discov-ered in this activity?**

● **What's good about not being like everybody else?**

Read aloud 1 Corinthians 12:12-27 and discuss the importance of differences. Ask kids to use the analogy in the Corinthians pas-sage to describe different people in the group. (Make sure all the comparisons are positive.)

GIANT KISS 14

For each person, cut out a 12-inch Hershey's Kiss shape from cardboard or posterboard. Have kids sit on the floor in a circle, write their names on their kisses, and then pass the kisses to their right. When kids receive someone else's kiss, have them write on it something "sweet" they've seen that person do or say. They can also write any positive characteristics they see in that person. Every few minutes, have kids pass the kisses to the right again.

Repeat the process until everyone has written on all the kisses and each person's kiss is being held by the person on his or her left. Have kids

wrap the kisses in aluminum foil before return-
ing them to their owners. Ask kids to take their
kisses home unopened and save them for a
time when they're in a "sour" mood or feeling
down. Then they can unwrap the kiss and be
encouraged by their friends' words.

15 GOOD-WILL BOOK

Select a member of your youth group each
week to be the recipient of a "good-will
book." During the week, have the other
members of the youth group each write a
personal letter to the person who was chosen to
receive the book. In their letters, ask kids to
include specific affirmations, encouragements, favorite verses, or any other positive personal messages they'd like to
share with the teenager. Bind the letters in a creatively decorated folder
with the teenager's name on it. Then
present the book to the teenager for
him or her to keep. Continue the practice
each week until all the members of the group
have received a good-will book.

HEAVEN'S MAILBOX

This is an activity that can be conducted over a whole season or even a school year.

Set aside an area in the youth group room or church entry to act as a small post office. Purchase or obtain a standard rural-roadside mailbox. Have kids customize it with painting or lettering, identifying it as "Heaven's Mailbox," "The Barnabas Box," or something similar. Provide envelopes and colored 3×5 cards for kids to write notes of praise or encouragement to each other.

Encourage kids to write affirming notes to one another during the week and place them in the box. Once a month, open the box and deliver the notes to kids. Add your own notes to assure each person receives encouraging words.

17 LOVE IS

Display a large heart-shape cookie with an inscription written in icing that reads, "God is love." Have your group sit in a circle with the cookie in the middle, while you read aloud 1 Corinthians 13.

Have group members take turns breaking off a piece of the cookie and giving it to someone else in the group as they explain one way they've seen God's love in that person. Tell kids that each person must receive a piece of cookie and that they may give a piece to more than one person. Place a three-minute time limit on each person's turn. When everyone has been affirmed, cut up the remainder of the cookie and divide it among the group. Pray together that God's love will continue to be evident in the lives of group members.

18 MARBLE MARVELS

Give kids each a marble and tell them their marbles represent the world. Have kids each describe *their* world by saying three words that tell why their world is wonderful and unique.

After all the kids have shared, tell them to find partners. Tell kids to each give away their "world" to their partner, while completing this statement: "You make my world a better place because you're..." Remind kids to say positive things such as "a caring person" or "understanding."

ME AND MY HOUSE

Tape a sheet of newsprint to the wall and set out markers. On the newsprint, have kids work together to create a floor plan for a super house. Be sure the house includes all the rooms common to a house and as many additional unique rooms as kids want.

Once the floor plan is complete, form a circle. Have kids each tell what room of this house best represents the person on their left and why. Then have them write that person's name in that room on the newsprint; for example, "Beth is like the kitchen because she's warm and cozy."

When everyone has been placed in the house, read aloud 1 Peter 2:4-5. Ask:

● **How is our youth group like a spiritual house?**

● **How can we make our house stronger?**

● **What rooms should be added to our house, if any?**

MORE THAN JUST HOT AIR

I f you have a young person who's sick or moving away, have your youth group write that student notes of encouragement on small slips of paper. Fold the slips so they can fit inside a balloon. After placing the notes in several balloons, fill the balloons with helium and make a bouquet. Have a group of kids deliver the balloons and cheer while the person pops the balloons and reads the notes.

MY DAILY AFFIRMATION

G ather enough baby food jars or old pill bottles for each person to have one. (If you can't find enough containers, use regular-size envelopes.) Also bring paper, tape, and pens.

Form groups of eight (or fewer). Give kids each a jar (or envelope) and have them cover the outside with paper. Have each person use a marker to label the jar "My Daily Affirmation."

Tell students they're going to fill each other's jars with enough affirmations to last a week.

Pass out one sheet of paper for each person. Have kids tear the paper into seven long strips.

On the strips of paper, have kids each write one encouraging note to each person in their group. (If your group has fewer than eight people, have some people write more than one affirmation to each person.) The encouragements can be anything from "You have a beautiful smile!" to "I appreciate the way you seek God." When each note is complete, have kids roll up and tape the strip of paper into a "pill" shape and put it in the appropriate group member's jar.

Tell kids to take their jars home. Instruct them to "take one affirmation per day and call God every morning" to help them feel better about themselves.

NOTES OF THE ROUND TABLE

For each person, cut out an 8-inch diameter paper circle (or use paper plates). Gather kids around a round table and give each person a circle and a pen. After kids write their names on their circles, have them slide their circles across the table. Have kids each take a different circle, read the name, and then write one "honorable" quality they see in that person.

After kids write a quality, have them slide the circle back across the table to someone new. Continue until everyone has written a note on every circle.

Return the circles to their owners and allow kids time to read them. Tape all the circles to one wall of the room and leave them up for several weeks as a constant encouragement to kids.

23 OBJECT LIKE ME

Form a circle. Have kids each choose an object in the room and, if possible, have them retrieve the object and hold it in their lap. One at a time, have kids stand in the center of the circle with their objects. While each person stands in the center, have group members tell positive ways that person's object is like him or her. For example, if someone chooses a chair, kids could say that person is good at helping other people rest and take it easy. Or, if someone chooses a piece of chalk, kids might say that person leaves her mark wherever she goes, or that his bubbly personality really rubs off on people.

PAT ON THE BACK 24

Give kids each a sheet of paper, a pencil, and tape. Have kids outline their handprints on the paper and then tape the sheet to their backs (with their friends' help).

Say: **You all deserve a pat on the back today—just because you're you. To show it, I want each of you to write on each person's back one special and specific reason that they deserve a "pat on the back." For example, you might list a recent accomplishment or a positive character trait.**

When everyone is finished, have kids read what their friends wrote. Tell kids to take home their sheets and refer to them any time they need a pat on the back.

PING PONG SHOWER 25

Purchase enough Ping Pong balls for approximately three per person. Prior to the meeting, use a permanent marker to write positive, descriptive characteristics of members of your group on the balls—one on each ball. Use words such as "caregiver," "peacemaker," "sweet singer," or "awesome artist."

Suspend the Ping Pong balls in a net or basket from a hook or light fixture in the room. Ask kids to sit close together on the floor under the balls. Explain that they'll soon be "showered with compliments," which they're supposed to share with their peers.

Drop the balls on kids' heads. Have kids each grab a Ping Pong ball, read what it says, and find someone to give that compliment to. For example, from a ball that reads "sweet singer," a young person could say, "Sherry, you're an awesome singer" and then give her that ball. Make sure no one receives more than three Ping Pong balls.

Have kids take home their Ping Pong balls as reminders of how awesome they are.

26 PRAY FOR ME

Form a circle. Tell kids they're going to pray for the person on their right. Have kids each complete this sentence aloud for the person on their right:

"I thank God for _____, because if we didn't have _____, we wouldn't have..." Ask kids to complete the prayer by naming a positive quality that person has; for example, "I thank God for Mike, because if we didn't have Mike, we wouldn't have a sense of humor."

Close the prayer time by completing this

prayer for the whole group: "I thank God for this youth group, because if we didn't have this youth group, we wouldn't have..."

For a variation on this activity, have people repeat in unison, "We thank God for _____ _____ because if we didn't have, _____ we wouldn't have..." Then call out positive affirmations for that person. Continue until each person has been affirmed by the group.

ROUND ROBIN

Buy plain postcards for each person in your group. Give each person a postcard and the address of someone else in the group. Have kids each write notes of encouragement to their assigned young person, along with something they like about that person. Tell kids to keep the cards anonymous. Collect the postcards and mail them. At the next meeting, have kids talk about how they felt when they got the postcard in the mail. Ask:

● **How does it feel to know that someone else has something good to say about you? Explain.**

● **Why is it important to feel wanted and liked?**

● **Why is it important to build up one another in our faith?**

● **How else can we build up one another in the coming weeks?**

Write kids' responses on newsprint and

choose several ways to build one another up over the next six weeks.

28 SEALED BLESSINGS

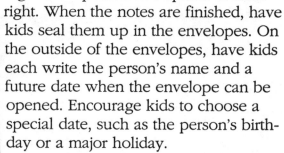

orm a circle and give kids each paper, a pen, and an envelope. On their paper, have kids each write a note of encouragement or a blessing for the person two spaces to their right. When the notes are finished, have kids seal them up in the envelopes. On the outside of the envelopes, have kids each write the person's name and a future date when the envelope can be opened. Encourage kids to choose a special date, such as the person's birthday or a major holiday.

Have kids each give their note to the appropriate person and tell them to save their encouraging notes until the date marked on the envelope.

 29 SPARKLERS

ather one sparkler for each person. If your city doesn't allow sparklers, use long matches or candles instead. Form a circle outside and go up to one person in the circle and complete this statement: **Your life sparkles because...**

After you complete your statement, light the person's sparkler and then have that person quickly complete the statement for another person in the circle. Continue until all the sparklers are lit.

Have kids raise their sparklers overhead and pray together, thanking God for adding his sparkle to their lives.

For a variation of this affirmation, form circles of no more than four and give each group a sparkler. Have kids light and pass the sparkler around the circle and complete the same statement for the person they're passing it to.

STICK IT TO ME 30

Give kids each a page of different types of stickers. The stickers could include words, such as "wow" or "super," or they could be full of fun pictures. It doesn't matter, as long as they're positive.

Tell kids to give their stickers away by sticking them on other group members. As kids give away their stickers, have them explain why they're giving a particular sticker to a particular person; for example, "I'm giving you this sticker of a lion because you always ferociously defend your friends."

Make sure the stickers are distributed evenly. After all the stickers have been given out, have kids each model their stickers for the whole group.

31 SWEET THOUGHTS OF YOU

Collect everyone's name in a basket. Have each person draw a name of someone in the group and write a note of encouragement about that person.

Say: **The only "catch" in writing your note of encouragement is that you must use as many candy bar names as you can. For example, "When you walk into a room, I sometimes think I hear a 'Symphony' " or "You're 'Mounds' of fun."**

Have kids each read what they wrote in their note. Give candy bar prizes to the people who use the most candy bar names.

TOILET PAPER TREASURES

Form a circle and pass around a roll of toilet paper, having kids each tear off at least five squares (they can tear off more if they want, just don't tell them what the squares are for).

Form groups of four. For each square kids have, ask them to say one thing they appreciate about the person to their right.

WANTED POSTERS

Take an instant-print picture of each person in your group. Tape the pictures on separate legal-size sheets of paper. Across the top of each sheet, write "WANTED." Tape the sheets along the walls of your meeting room.

Provide markers and have kids go around the room writing on each poster one reason why that person is "wanted" by the youth group. Make sure kids understand that all the wanted statements need to be positive and affirming; for example, "Jeff is wanted because he always cheers people up."

When all the posters are finished, let kids take theirs home as a reminder that they'll always be "wanted" in the youth group.

34

WATER THAT REFRESHES

Form a circle and give each person a clear, plastic cup. Hold up a pitcher of water and tell kids they're going to refresh one another with the water of friendship. Fill one cup with water and then join the circle.

Without mentioning any names, tell how one person in the group has blessed you with his or her friendship. After you've shared, go over to the person you were talking about and fill his or her cup with water by emptying out your own cup. As you do, say: **You have refreshed me with your friendship. Thank you.**

Have group members continue the process until everyone has had his or her cup filled at least once. Then fill everyone's cup with water and pray together, asking God to help kids always be a source of refreshment for one another. Drink the water together as a symbol of the group's unity and support.

YOU ARE WHAT YOU WEAR

Have each person bring a plain T-shirt or sweatshirt to the meeting. Have kids put their names on the shirts with a piece of tape. Distribute several colors of permanent markers. Lay out the shirts and have kids go around and write positive qualities about each person on his or her shirt. Make sure that each person goes to several shirts and that all of the shirts are written on by several people.

When everyone is finished, return the shirts to their owners. Read aloud 2 Corinthians 4:16-18 and ask:

● **Do you believe the saying, "The clothes make the man (or woman)"? Why or why not?**

● **How do our outward actions— our dress and attitudes—reflect what we think of ourselves on the inside?**

Have kids put on their shirts or sweatshirts. Ask:

● **How does it feel to wear these shirts that reflect the positive inner qualities others see in you?**

● **What can you do to make your inner qualities more evident than your outward ones?**

PART 2

TEENAGERS TO OTHERS

AFFIRMATIONS FOR TEENAGERS TO GIVE TO OTHERS

ADOPT A CLASS 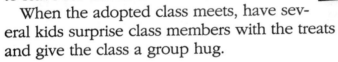 36

Have youth group members adopt a Sunday school class or other organization in your church such as the choir or the senior's club.

During a midweek youth meeting, have kids decorate the adopted class's meeting room with balloons, streamers, and banners. Fill the banners with positive statements, such as "You're awesome!" or "We love you." Obtain a class roll and have kids make cards for each member with encouraging statements. Have volunteers bake cookies or brownies to leave for the class.

When the adopted class meets, have several kids surprise class members with the treats and give the class a group hug.

ADOPT A GRANDPARENT 37

Get a list of shut-ins and active senior citizens from the church office. Make sure you collect only names of people who would welcome being "adopted" by a teenager.

Form pairs and assign each pair a "grandparent" for them to adopt for the next week. During that week, have pairs contact their grandparent, explain what the youth group is doing, and offer a list of possible activities pairs can do for their grandparent. The list might include activities such as taking grandparents to lunch, taking them for a drive, helping them around the house, running errands for them, getting their groceries, or just visiting with them.

At the end of the week, have pairs work together to write a thank you note to their adopted grandparent, thanking him or her for the opportunity to serve.

The next Sunday, form new pairs and assign a new batch of grandparents to kids for them to serve that week. Continue the process until all the senior citizens in your church have been adopted at least once.

38 ADOPT A MISSIONARY

Have the group choose a missionary or a missionary family to adopt for one year. Use these questions to set youth group goals for the year:

● **How much financial support will we send over the next year?**

● **How many letters will we write to the missionaries?**

● **What creative things will we do for holidays or other special occasions?**

● **How will we organize our commitment to pray for the missionaries?**

At the end of the year, videotape a celebration in honor of the missionaries and mail it to them.

ANGELS UNAWARE

Ask each of your young people to identify someone at school who doesn't attend any church. For the 12 weeks, have kids each commit to becoming that person's "undercover angel."

Weekly, have kids each slip a card into their person's locker at school, leave a gift for him or her in the office, write a note of encouragement after a poor grade, or offer some other kind of secret encouragement. Each week in the youth group meeting, have kids each report on what they did and what their person's reaction has been. Weekly reports will help keep the motivation and interest high.

After 12 weeks, kids can choose a new person to reach out to. Encourage kids *not* to reveal themselves to their secret person, even after they've moved on to a new person. Tell them to make this ministry something that's "just between me and God."

40

BANNER AFFIRMATIONS

Have kids create fun banners for various staff members in the church, such as janitors, secretaries, and pastors. On the banners, have kids include drawings, notes of appreciation, and messages of encouragement.

Each week, have kids secretly "plant" a banner in a place where the intended person will discover it. For example, if kids make a banner for the janitor, have them place it in the broom closet.

41

BIG BROTHER . . . BIG SISTER

At one of your next youth outings, have kids each pick an elementary-age child to go along as their special pal. Encourage the youth group to work on making the younger kids feel important and respected. Tell them to focus their conversation on the younger kids and strive to encourage them.

Choose an activity that can be fun for both age groups—not something that will make younger kids feel inadequate. Some good ideas are going to a video arcade, going to eat pizza, or going out for a movie and ice cream.

CHRISTMAS GIFT-AWAY

D uring the Christmas season this year, have your youth group sponsor a Christmas gift list for young children in a nearby hospital, orphanage, detention center, or disadvantaged apartment complex or neighborhood. On a Saturday or Sunday afternoon, five weeks before Christmas, have the youth group canvas one of these groups of children and learn what *personal* gifts they'd appreciate.

If your focus is in a neighborhood, have kids go door to door, meet the parent, and explain what they're doing. Then have kids ask the parent for gift suggestions for children in that home. If your focus is children in a hospital or orphanage, have kids ask the staff for suggestions for each child.

Have kids set up a Christmas tree in the entry area of the church building. Place tags on the tree that describe each gift the group needs. Church members can review the tags, choose a gift they will bring, and place it with the tag under the tree.

Encourage church members to purchase the suggested gifts so members of your group can experience giving something meaningful to another person.

A few days before Christmas, have group members deliver the gifts to each child in person. After Christmas, have kids phone the parents or the hospital staff to make sure all the gifts were in good condition and well-received.

43 CHURCH LEADER APPRECIATION

Have your group throw a party for your church leaders.

To prepare for this party, form three groups. Have group 1 be responsible for making and sending invitations, arranging for the food, and decorating. Have group 2 take care of writing letters of appreciation to each church leader and delivering them to the leaders at the party. Have group 3 use tape recorders to interview members of the congregation as they tell what they appreciate most about various leaders. Play back these recordings at the party.

Close the party with a circle of prayer, thanking God for the leadership, commitment, and example of your church leaders.

MIRROR MESSAGES

44

Have kids make mirror decorations for your church bathrooms and kids' homes. Provide kids with fine-point markers and various sizes and colors of blank self-stick notes. Have kids write positive statements, such as "You look great today" or "Smile, God loves you," or a Bible passage on the notes and decorate them with flowers or little characters. Then send kids to all the bathrooms in the church and have them stick the notes on the mirrors.

Take all the extra sticky notes and lead kids on a "house raid." Drive kids to one of their friends' homes and have kids do a quick raid on the home—placing the sticky notes on every bathroom mirror in the house.

NURSING HOME PHOTOS

45

Gather kids together for a group photograph. Enlarge the photo to 5×7 or 8×10 and make several framed copies. Each month, have group members form groups

of no more than four and write encouraging notes to different patients in a nearby nursing home (you'll need to collect the names and assign them to kids).

After all the notes are written, take kids to the nursing home to deliver their notes, along with the framed photographs of the youth group. The next month, have groups each write to a different person in the nursing home. Continue for several months, until everyone in the nursing home has received a note and a framed photograph of the group.

46 PARENT DATE NIGHT

Have your group plan a special "date night" for youth parents. Have kids make and send invitations ahead of time and then have teenagers and sponsors prepare a nice candlelight dinner at the church. Provide soft music and entertainment during dinner.

At some point in the evening, have kids publicly express their appreciation for their parents and thank them for all they've done on the kids' behalf.

Be sure to provide babysitting for younger siblings and make a point to include single parents or those whose spouses cannot attend.

PIZZA PHANTOMS

A sk kids to be on the lookout at school for any friends of theirs who may be going through a rough time. Ask kids to quietly compile a list of people who need encouragement and give it to you along with the students' addresses.

Then, after a youth group meeting, send kids in groups on "pizza raids" to the homes of the various people kids selected. Have kids raid a house (make sure they're home) by dropping pizza at the door, ringing the door bell, and running away. Have all the groups leave a printed message that reads, "You are LOVED!" along with group members' names.

SECRETARY PRAISE

A ssign a secret task force of young people to find ways to creatively affirm the secretaries who work in your church office. Kids might leave special messages on the church's answering machine, type "You are special" on the computer screen while the secretary is away from the desk, or send flowers for no reason except to say, "We love you. Signed, the Youth Group."

49 SERVANT DAY

Have teenagers each choose a day to become a servant for their family. Have kids tell parents they're doing this as a way of saying, "I love you." Have kids do tasks that their parents assign—tasks that go beyond their daily required chores. Parents can give their teenager a list of chores to do, such as washing dishes, doing the laundry, ironing, doing yard work, shopping for groceries, washing the cars, or car pooling younger siblings to activities.

At the next youth meeting, have teenagers share their experiences and their feelings about their "servant" day. Have kids each write a letter to their parents to thank them for the hard work they do as parents.

SPECIAL RESERVATIONS

Set aside a small section of seats in your auditorium or sanctuary near where the youth group normally sits. Designate those seats as "love seats." Each week, have the youth group pick a person from the congregation who has in some way been a help, a support, or just a good example to kids in the group.

That Sunday, when that special person comes in the door, have kids standing ready to intercept him or her. Have kids explain that he or she has been chosen to sit in the youth group's love seat that Sunday. Have kids also explain why that person was chosen.

When the person sits in the love seat, have kids crowd around him or her and offer lots of hugs.

THANKS A BUNCH!

Have kids choose a pastor, layperson, or parent in the church who has been especially meaningful to the youth group. For that person, construct a super-size card by folding a sheet of poster-board in half. Have kids decorate the card. Then have each young person write a note of encouragement or gratitude on the card. When the card is filled with encouragements, have kids deliver it.

"WE LOVE YOU, PASTOR" PARTY

Have the youth group invite the pastor and his or her family to a small party—but have kids secretly invite the entire church! Surprise the pastor with banners, posters, balloons, and thank you gifts from people throughout the congregation.

Have the youth group provide entertainment with skits, songs, and games. Include as part of your activities a time when the pastor sits in front of the group and listens to people explain why they appreciate him or her.

PART 3

LEADER TO TEENAGERS

AFFIRMATIONS FOR LEADERS TO GIVE TO TEENAGERS

BEDROOM PROFILE

53

I n your youth newsletter, include a column called the "Bedroom Profile." In this column, get permission to write a descriptive profile of a particular young person's bedroom. Include descriptions of the posters, the type of music in the room, the names of any books that may be present, and an overall description of the room's details.

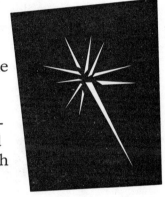

Write a new profile for each issue of the newsletter and make sure all the profiles you include are positive. At the end of each profile, include a paragraph describing how special that young person is and why he or she is appreciated by the youth group.

BIBLE BLASTERS

54

O n separate postcards, write several different encouraging scripture passages for your kids. Each week, send a few scripture postcards out to kids along with a brief message of encouragement, such as "I think you're great!" or "Hang in there!"

Continue sending out the postcards each week until each group member has received one.

55 CANDLE AFFIRMATION

Form a circle and give each person a candle. Light your candle and hold it up. Then go around the circle and light each candle. As you do, tell each person one way he or she has brought light into your life. When all the candles are lit, lead the group in a prayer, thanking God for letting you see so much of the beauty he sees in your group members.

56 CARE COUPONS

Create a series of coupons to hand out to kids over a four-week period as they come into youth meetings. The coupons can be for anything that encourages kids; for example, "This coupon is good for a free hug," "This coupon is good for lunch," or "This coupon is good for a time of prayer together."

Encourage kids to redeem the coupons by calling you at the church and arranging a time to get together.

CREATIVE WITHIN LIMITS

O nce a month, have a group of no more than six kids run an activity for the youth group. The activity could be a social with games and refreshments or a time of worship with music, singing, and prayer. Kids could even organize an outreach event featuring a band of musicians from the youth group.

Whatever the activity, give kids a specific idea of what you're expecting. Allow them the freedom to be creative within the limits you set. Meet with them during the planning stages and make yourself available to help in any way.

When the activity is over, take the planning group out for ice cream to congratulate them on their efforts. Tell each member at least one positive quality you saw in him or her during the planning and leading of this event.

58

GIFTS OF SELF-ESTEEM

As a youth group leader, you'll have many opportunities to give gifts to young people for occasions such as confirmation, birthdays, graduations, or farewells. Consider the following esteem-building gift ideas:

● **a set of personalized note pads that say, "You are awesome!";**

● **a bookmark or plaque that includes the young person's name, the name's meaning, and a Bible passage;**

● **personalized stationery embossed with the person's name and address;**

● **a plain T-shirt that the group decorates with permanent markers or puff paints; or**

● **a mug or key chain engraved with a personal message from the youth group.**

I'M PROUD TO BE YOUR LEADER

59

Place pictures of your youth group members—individuals and group shots—on your refrigerator at home or on your bulletin board at church. This way, every time your kids drop by, they'll see how special they are to you.

LIVING LABELS

60

Send a note to each of your group members, telling them each about a special Bible verse you picked for them and why you think it's so appropriate to them. Call the verse a living label, explaining that you hope they'll wear the verse as a label for their lives. For example, you might choose 1 Peter 1:5, "God's power protects you through your faith..." for someone who deals with lots of struggles at school.

Memorize the verses you choose for each person and remind kids of their living label whenever you get an opportunity.

61 McDONALD'S BY CANDLELIGHT

Host a candlelight dinner at McDonald's for your youth group. Reserve a special section of the restaurant for your group. Take along tablecloths, candles, and someone to serve as a waiter. As kids enjoy their food, offer a soft drink toast to them that expresses how much you love and care for them as a group.

62 MARKED FOR JESUS

Lead a meeting that focuses on the crucifixion of Jesus. As a part of the meeting, go around the room and use a marker to draw a cross on each person's palm. As you draw the cross, tell the person one quality you see in him or her that you believe Jesus finds valuable enough to die for. Then thank the person for letting you see that quality, too.

MODERN ART AUCTION

Go to the library and check out several books of paintings and find out what the paintings are worth. At your meeting, distribute blank paper and colored markers. Have kids make their own "paintings."

When they're finished, hold a mock auction with a few of the art pieces. Then show the students copies of some of the art you found at the library. Have them guess how much was paid for the pieces.

Ask:

● **What makes this art so valuable?**

Say: **This art is valuable because of the skills of the artist and because someone out there is willing to pay such a huge price for it.**

Ask:

● **How are you like a piece of art?**

● **How much was Jesus willing to pay to get you?**

● **Based on what Jesus has done, what is your value compared to this art? to anything else on the planet? to anything in the universe?**

Read aloud Romans 5:6-8. Say: **You have been bought with a price, and that price was higher than the cost of any other thing in the universe. That makes you the most valuable thing in this universe—outside of God himself.**

Close with prayer, asking God to help kids see how valuable they are to him.

NAME GAME

Go through a book that contains a listing of names and their meanings and choose new names for each person in your youth group. Make your choices by matching kids' positive qualities with the meanings of the names in the book.

Bring the book to your youth group. Ask group members to each select a new name for themselves based on the name's meaning—not how it sounds.

Once kids have chosen their new names, have them each say their new name and explain why they chose it. Then go around the room and tell kids the name you chose for each of them. Explain why you chose each name and then offer a sentence prayer for each person, asking God to draw out more of the beauty you see in each of them.

65

OLYMPIC AWARDS

Create an "Olympic" medal for each person in your group. On each medal, write that person's name, special qualities, and the things you particularly like about him or her.

In a special ceremony (complete with fanfare music such as the theme from *Rocky,* the Olympic theme, or "Fanfare for the Common Man" by Aaron Copeland), present kids with their medals. Tell kids each why you're giving them their medal and explain that the medals are not just tokens of praise—they're also symbols of your commitment to love each young person unconditionally.

PHOTO PRAISE 66

Have double prints made when you have film developed from youth group activities. Then write notes on the backs of the photos to the kids in the pictures. Tell kids how much you enjoy their being a part of your group.

SALTY JEWELRY 67

Jesus said, "You are the salt of the earth" (Matthew 5:13). Lead a meeting that focuses on Christians as the salt of the earth. As a part of the meeting, make necklaces using string tied around chunks of rock salt as jewels. Give a necklace to each person. As you hand out the gifts, tell kids each one way they demonstrate that they're the salt of the earth.

68 SIGNS OF KINDNESS

During a meeting of your volunteer leaders and parents, make colorful, sturdy posters for each young person in your group. On each poster, include the student's name and encouraging statements, such as "Shelly is Special to First Church Youth Group." Make the statements large enough to be seen at a distance.

After the meeting, have parents and volunteers take the posters to kids' homes and post them in their yards.

69 STAR OF THE WEEK

Each Sunday, choose a member of the youth group to be the Star of the Week. Have a Star of the Week bulletin board set up in the meeting room. The week before their turn, ask kids' parents to write a small biography about their teenager. Ask them to include a listing of family members, friends, their teenagers' likes and dislikes, hobbies, talents, strengths, and career goals.

On Sunday morning, display the biography on the Star of the Week bulletin board, along with a fun photograph from a recent youth event. During Sunday school, introduce the Star. Read the biography and tell a few reasons you think the Star is worth being a Star.

During the following week, send the Star a special note in the mail, take him or her to dinner, or do something fun together.

TEENAGER TIME

Choose a 15-minute period each day that you'll block out to concentrate on the kids in your group. On Monday, pray for your teenagers during that time. On Tuesday, call one or more of the kids just to let them know you're thinking of them and that you appreciate them. On Wednesday, drop a few postcards in the mail to other group members, telling them how valuable they are to God and to you. Offer to give a group of kids a ride home from school or ball practice on Thursday, just so you can have a few minutes to chat together. On Friday, look for a news item or

some other bit of information that would interest your kids and save it to post on the youth bulletin board the following Sunday.

The young people in your group will know you think they're special when they see evidence that they're on your mind all week long.

THIS SONG'S FOR YOU

As a way to encourage kids and get them interested in Christian music, choose a special contemporary Christian song for each group member that in some way highlights a positive quality he or she has.

At a special meeting, play each song and explain to each person why you chose the particular song you did. Describe the qualities you see in that person that are reflected in the song.

WRITE-A-THON

Write a personal note to each of your group members, mentioning several things you appreciate about him or her. Do this every day for one week. If you have a large group, write notes to half the group one day and the other half the next day. Don't tell kids what you're doing.

At your next meeting, ask:

● **How did it feel to receive the encouraging notes this week?**

● **After you received the first few notes, did you start anticipating more? Why or why not?**

Have kids read Hebrews 10:24-25 and talk about different ways they can help to build up those around them. Challenge them to try some of their ideas during the coming week.

PART 4

GROUP BUILDERS

AFFIRMATIONS
FOR BUILDING
COMMUNITY IN
YOUR GROUP

Give each member of your group several balloons and a marker. Ask for volunteers to share stories of times in their lives when they felt they were needed or when they helped someone else. Every time the rest of the kids hear the storyteller mention a way that he or she helped someone else, or had a kind attitude toward someone, have them blow a breath of air into their balloons.

When the story is done, have kids each tie off their balloon, write the storyteller's name on it, and write on it the good qualities they noted about the person during the story. Tie all the balloons together and give them to the storyteller as a balloon bouquet.

"CLAY NEEDS YOU" 74
DEVOTION

Plan a devotion around the theme of self-esteem by using a fictitious character named Clay Thompson, who is represented by a lump of clay that you hold in your hand. Throughout the devotion, hold out the lump of clay for the group to see.

Say: **Clay is a talented guy. He plays in the band at his high school.** (Roll the ball of clay in your hand.) **He gets good grades and is popular with guys and girls. Recently his dad moved out of the house. Things at home became sad and depressing.** (Pull off a little bit of clay and hand it to someone in the front.) **After his dad left, Clay didn't feel like doing his homework. He'd just close the door to his room and listen to music. His grades started to drop.** (Pull off another piece of clay and hand it to another person.) **Clay didn't practice his saxophone, so when tryouts came he moved down four chairs.** (Pull off another piece of clay and give it to a third person.) **Clay's best friend, Seth, noticed something was wrong. "Hey, what's up, Clay?" he asked. "You're acting weird lately." Clay looked down and said, "Things are bad at home. My dad moved out." Seth simply mumbled, "That's too bad,"** and walked away. (Pull off another piece of clay and hand it to someone.) **When Clay returned home from school that day, his mom was sitting on the front step waiting for him. "We need to talk, Clay," said his mother sadly. "Your father and I are getting a divorce." Clay was crushed.** (Flatten the lump of clay with your fist.)

Stop the story here and ask the group to finish the story with ways to build Clay back up again. Have people hand you their pieces of clay as they offer their suggestions. As they tell their stories, roll Clay back into a complete ball again.

After the devotion, give kids each a small ball of clay. Form groups of three and have kids tell their group members about times they've felt like Clay. Have kids each encourage their group members by telling them how awesome they are and how worthy they are of love—from God and others. Each time someone shares an encouragement, have him or her give the encouraged person a piece of clay. Close by having kids pray for one another.

GROUP COMMERCIAL

F orm teams of five or six. If possible, include an adult sponsor on each team. Have each team create a 30-second TV commercial advertising your youth group. Allow them 15 minutes to discuss the positive aspects of the youth group and to design the commercial. Give them another 15 minutes to rehearse. Then have them perform their commercials for the rest of the youth group. Award a prize to the team with the best commercial. If possible, videotape the teams as they do their commercials and then play back the tape while kids enjoy refreshments. You can also play the tape again at future events to actually promote the youth group.

GROUP THEME SONG

Form teams of four to six. Give each team a list of the names of all the kids in the youth group. Have teams each pick a popular song and change the words. The new song should mention the names of as many group members as possible—and should say something encouraging about each person it mentions. Make sure all kids' names are represented in the songs.

When teams are ready, have them perform their songs in front of the whole group. The team that mentions the most names wins. After the songs are finished, ask:

● **Whose name did you listen for the most? Why?**

● **Why is praise from others so important?**

● **Which is better—being praised by a group of your close friends or by a group of strangers? Explain.**

LIFT AND ROCK

Ask kids to each bring a recording of a song they believe describes them or tells something important about their life. Take turns playing the songs—or play one per meeting for several weeks until everyone's song has been played.

While a person's song is playing, have the rest of the group members lift and rock him or her over their heads. Do this by having kids gather around the person (who's lying on the floor), pick the person up in their arms, and sway him or her to the music. Kids may laugh and act silly, but the message still gets through: "You're important to us!"

LIVING HISTORY COLLAGE

In a special corner, bookshelf, or selected area of your youth room, prepare a space for a growing memorial to the youth group's shared life through the group's common activities.

Each time kids go on a particular outing, missions effort, or other activity, have them bring back a small object to symbolize that experience. Date the objects and place them in the designated space to create a growing collage of experiences that reminds kids how special the group is. Examples might include a paddle or rock from a raft trip, a jar of sand from a beach trip, a brick from a missions trip, a branch from a hike, or a symbolic token from a retreat.

79 MANY FLAVORS... ONE SUNDAE

Take kids on a trip to a local ice cream parlor. Order the largest treat they have on the menu and have the group members share it. While kids eat, have them pick a different flavor of ice cream that best represents each person in the group. Make sure they explain why they chose a flavor for a particular person.

After all the flavors have been chosen, direct kids' attention to their ice cream treat. Ask:

● **How do all the "flavors" in our youth group work together to create a massive, delicious "treat"?**

"MEET THE YOUTH GROUP" SHOW

To help the rest of the church see how awesome your youth group is, sponsor a "meet the youth group" show for the congregation. Set it up like a fashion show, with background music and an announcer who reads from a sheet that kids each prepare beforehand. Have kids each complete an information sheet that contains items such as name, age, school, parents' names, other relatives who attend your church, best friend's name, hobbies, favorite subject in school, and lifelong goals.

At the end of the show, have kids line up on stage so church members can come up and hug them, say a kind word, or even pray for them individually.

MYSTERY WORD

Select a member from your group who needs special encouragement or attention. Let the others in the group know that this person will be specially—but secretly—recognized and loved in the next group meeting. Make sure no one tells the person what's going on.

Find out what kind of cake he or she likes and one gift that's deeply needed or appreciat-

ed. Hide these in the meeting room.

Pick a word or phrase that has something to do with your special person. For instance, for a baseball player you might use the phrase "hit a home run," or for a good student you might use the word "grades." Let everyone else know what the mystery word is.

During the meeting, have kids try to get the person to say the mystery word, without actually saying it themselves. When the person says the word, have all the kids cheer and start the party. Eat cake, give your gifts, and honor the group member.

ONE-MINUTE MISSIONARY

Form groups of three. Assign one person in each group to be the "blesser" and the other two to be "servants." Have the blessers think of a fun task for their servants to do that encourages someone else in the room. For example, the blesser might send the servants to rub someone's back, give someone a long hug, or stand next to someone and applaud him or her. The only catch is that the task must be completed within one minute.

Once the blessers have thought of their task, have them send off their servants to carry it out. After one minute, have the servants return to their groups. Have kids switch roles by assigning a new blesser in each group. Then have the new blesser come up with a task for the servants to do.

Continue this process until everyone has had several chances to be the blesser.

For a fast-paced variation on this activity, have the blessers each choose many different short "missions" to send their servants on during the one-minute time limit.

OUR PLACE

Have the youth group choose a restaurant or fast-food place in town to adopt as "our place." Once the location is chosen, go to the owners of the business and explain that the youth group has adopted it as its own. Reserve a special section of the restaurant and have a celebration that focuses on why the youth group is a great place to belong.

Go with kids to the restaurant often, as a reminder that the group is special and that every person in it has a place to belong.

PARENT LETTER

Ask parents to each write a letter to their teenager that lists all the positive qualities they see in him or her. Collect the letters and take them to a youth meeting.

At the meeting, read aloud each letter, without naming the parents or the teenager. After you read each letter, have kids guess which group member the letter was about. After they guess, have kids explain what things the letter said that "gave it away."

Give the letter to the appropriate teenager. Encourage all the kids to thank their parents for writing the letters.

Be sensitive to homes with indifferent parents. You may need to teach some parents how to give affirmations.

PASS THE FRUIT, PLEASE

Form groups of five and give each group a piece of fruit, such as an apple or an orange. Read aloud Galatians 5:22-23. On "go," have kids pass the fruit from person to person. On "stop," have the person holding the fruit remain quiet while the rest of his or her group tells about times they have seen that person show love. After a few minutes, signal kids to pass the fruit again.

Have kids stop again. This time have the person holding the fruit remain quiet while the rest of the group tells about times they saw that person demonstrate joy.

Continue this process until you've gone through all the fruit of the Spirit, and every person in the group has been encouraged.

Have kids share and eat the fruit. Then ask:

● **What does the fruit of a person's life tell us about him or her?**

● **Based on what we've shared today, what kind of group are we?**

Have kids give themselves a round of applause for bearing good fruit for God.

PEP RALLY

Say: **We have a lot to cheer about in our youth group. Tonight we're going to celebrate the things that make our group special.**

Form groups of five to eight. Give each group a sheet of paper, a pen, posterboard, and markers. Have groups each brainstorm a list of things that make their youth group special and write them on the paper.

After groups have listed several good qualities, instruct the groups to each pick one or two items from their list and create a cheer that communicates this quality. Have groups each write their cheer on posterboard so they can teach it to everyone. Encourage groups to create motions to go along with the cheers.

Have groups take turns presenting their cheers.

POSTER PUZZLE PUT-TOGETHER

Get a poster of a beautiful scene. Cut the poster into puzzle-shaped pieces—enough so that each group member can have a piece. Distribute the pieces along with markers and have kids each write their name on the back of their puzzle piece.

Have kids pass around the puzzle pieces. On the back of each one, have kids write what they like about the person the piece belongs to. Once everyone is finished, have kids assemble the puzzle-poster on the floor so that all the affirmations are showing (picture-side down). Allow kids each to read what other people wrote about them.

Then have kids reassemble the poster with the picture showing.

Ask:

● **How are the encouraging words on one side like this picture on the other side?**

● **How does our love for one another make us like a completed puzzle?**

● **Why are we each a vital piece of the puzzle in our youth group?**

ROUNDS OF APPLAUSE

88

Form groups of five to seven. Have groups each form a circle and place a chair in the center of their circle. One at a time, have group members stand on the chair for 20 to 30 seconds. While they stand on the chair, have the rest of the group erupt in rip-roaring applause. Encourage kids to be loud and not to stop cheering until the person's time is up. Continue until everyone has been cheered.

89 SENIORS PARTY

Have your youth group throw a special party for all your graduating seniors. Have kids each write encouraging notes on super-sized cards for each senior. Include in the evening a "blessing time" in which kids take turns telling individual seniors how they've had an impact on the group and on kids' lives.

As a part of your evening, take the seniors aside one at a time and videotape them offering words of encouragement to future youth group members. Keep these recordings on file and play them for new youth group members when they join.

90 SHOW AND TELL ABOUT SOMEONE ELSE

Set up a bulletin board titled "Show and Tell About Someone Else." When a person accomplishes something noteworthy, such as making an A on an exam or writing an award-winning story in a creative writing class, encourage group members to fill out a form that explains the details of the person's accomplishment.

Post the completed forms on the Show and Tell board and announce new additions to the board each week at your youth meetings.

SONGS FOR CLUSTERS

Form groups of three or four and have each group write a song or rap for a different group in the room. Tell groups they can use a popular tune or make one up of their own. The only rules are that the song or rap must mention the names of each person in the other group, and it must tell positive traits about each person in the other group.

When groups are ready, have them each perform their song or rap. Applaud each group's efforts. Have groups write the lyrics of their songs or raps on newsprint and tape them to the meeting room wall.

STAR-GAZING ESTEEM-BUILDER

Cut out several large, paper stars—enough so each group member can have one. Number the stars and beside each number write the name of a different young person in your group.

Tape the stars to the ceiling so that they spell out a significant attribute of your group, such as "love," "joy," "fun," or "unity." If your group isn't large enough to form a word with the stars, add more than one star for each person.

Give kids each a flashlight (or have them bring their own). Tell kids to lie on their backs on the floor as you turn out the lights.

Say: **Each one of you is a star in some way that shines for Jesus. And your star is an important part of the constellation of our group. You're needed to make us complete. Look into the skies using your flashlights and find** (any group member's name)**'s star(s).**

When all lights are shining on the first star, have kids tell how that person shines for God in

their group. Continue calling out group members' names until kids have found all the stars and talked about all the members of the group. Then ask:

● **Who can guess what our group's constellation spells out?**

See if anyone can figure it out. Turn on the lights, have everyone sit up, and discuss why that word describes the uniqueness of how your group shines for Jesus.

STUCK IN THE MIDDLE WITH YOU

Purchase or obtain a 6-inch Velcro fastener (the self-stick kind) for each person in your group. Lead a meeting on commitments and "sticking together" as a family.

As a part of the meeting, have kids apply the sticky side of the Velcro to the outsides of their legs two feet up from the floor. Tell kids to apply the "gripper" side to their left legs and the fuzzy side to their right legs.

Tell kids to close their eyes. Without opening their eyes, have kids each find two people to stick to by matching Velcro pieces. Continue until the entire group is stuck together in a circle. Then have kids each tell why they're glad to be a part of the youth group and how they'll commit to "stick together" with the group in the future.

94 TEETER, TOTTER, YOU MATTER!

Take the kids to a playground for a fun time of childlike play. As a part of the fun, have kids gather around the teeter-totter. Place two group members on the teeter-totter and have them go at it. Each time a person is raised into the air, have the group members call out one childlike quality that person has that the group appreciates; for example, "playfulness," "kindness," or "honesty." Allow each person about four or five affirmations before letting a new set of kids get on the teeter-totter. Continue until all the kids have been encouraged by the group.

95 THANKS FOR THE MEMORIES

Read aloud Psalm 136. Have kids each write their own history from birth to the present in 10 events or less—including both good times and hard times. Between each major event, have kids write this paraphrase from Psalm 136: "God's love lasts forever."

Here's an example:

I was born a healthy baby in Texas.

God's love lasts forever.

My mom and dad divorced when I was five.

God's love lasts forever.

My mom and I moved to Seattle, where I grew up next to the ocean.

God's love lasts forever.

When kids are finished, have them each read aloud their history. After each person reads, have the group applaud him or her and offer hugs to congratulate this person for making it this far.

THANKSGIVING IN JANUARY

96

P lan this activity for a night in January when your kids think they're coming to a regular youth group meeting or Bible study. Several weeks before the meeting, get together with a few parents and adult leaders to plan a Thanksgiving dinner for the youth group. Plan a traditional meal of turkey with all the trimmings—gravy, potatoes, and pumpkin pie.

Have one of the parents make a banner that says, "We thank God for our kids!" Have the parents provide slides of the kids at different ages. Make a cassette tape of different parents and youth leaders saying positive things about the youth

group. Play the tape and show the slides as entertainment for the night.

At some point in the evening, explain to kids that this event is just a way of saying thanks to them for being who they are and letting them know they're loved!

97 THIRTY SECONDS OF PRAISE

Have kids gather in a dark room and form a circle. Using a flashlight, "spotlight" one person in the group for 30 seconds. During that time, have kids race to say things they appreciate about that person and tell why they're glad that person is a part of the group.

Every 30 seconds, switch to a different person. Continue until everyone has been spotlighted—including yourself!

TOOL TIME

Bring to your youth group meeting a tool-box containing a wide variety of tools. Form groups of no more than five and give each group a sheet of paper and a pencil. Have each group take a tool from the toolbox. Challenge groups to list ways that the good aspects of your youth group are like the tool they selected; for instance, "Our youth group is like this hammer because it helps us to penetrate our world with the gospel the way a hammer helps a nail penetrate wood." After groups are finished, have them share their analogies with the rest of the youth group. Have groups get back together for a time of prayer, asking God to help them continue to build a great youth group.

WITNESS STAND

Set up a makeshift witness stand in your meeting room. Each week, put a different group member "on trial" and ask for witnesses to take the stand to explain why that person is a valuable part of the youth group. Allow several short testimonies before declaring that person "totally accepted and loved" by the youth group.

YOU DECORATED MY LIFE

Form groups of four. Provide assorted decorations and makeup items and tell kids their job is to decorate each person in their group. Explain that the decorations must each reflect some positive quality that person has. For example, kids might tape a paper sun to a person's head to indicate that the person "shines" in the youth group.

After everyone has been decorated, conduct a fashion show, having group members each explain the decorations they choose.

YOUTH GROUP CANNISTER

Collect several Pringles potato chip tubes (or create similar tubes with stiff paper and tape). Cover the cannisters with specially designed sheets of paper that say, "You Are Special!" Include the name of your group, your meeting times, and your location. Make each cannister colorful and attractive.

Ask kids to each write a few sentences explaining why your group is a good place to belong, as well as their desire to have others join the group. Photocopy these notes and place a copy in each cannister. Include a letter from you, telling what you appreciate about the group.

When the cannisters are complete, give one to each person in your group. Also make several extras for kids to hand out to friends who they want to invite to join the youth group.

CONTRIBUTORS

Many thanks to the following people, who loaned us their expertise to help create this volume of ideas:

Beth Rowland
Byron Kehler
Carol and Gary Wilde
Christina Medina
Christine Yount
Jamie Snodgrass
Jennifer Wilger
Jody Wakefield
Karen Ceckowski
Lianne Bauserman
Margaret Hinchey
Michael Warden
Mike Nappa
Rex Stepp
Ron and Janette Stinnett
Steve and Cindy Parolini
Steve Huddleston
Susan Rigby
Thom and Joani Schultz
Wes Olds